Working Here

David Salner

Rooster Hill Press

Mankato, Minnesota   2010

Copyright 2010

All rights reserved. Except for brief quotations in critical articles or reviews, no part of this book may be reproduced in any manner without prior written permission from the publisher: **Rooster Hill Press,** 230 Armstrong Hall, Minnesota State University, Mankato, Minnesota, 56001.

First Edition

ISBN#: 978-0-557-50896-9

Contest Judges:

    Candace Black, Jorge Evans, Roger Sheffer

Rooster Hill interns:

    Caitlin O'Sullivan, Alex Phillips

Cover Photo: The Rotary Kiln at Eveleth Mines, Minnesota

Dedications:

*For John and Mabel Langford and in memory of
Alejandro Langford (1983-2010)*

For Lily and Paul Bisson

*For Barbara – this book is not the most important thing
your love makes possible*

Working Here   Contents

I. First check

First Check   9
Swimming the Severn   11
As Far As He Dared   12
The Welder on Midnight Shift   13
Manhattan Seasons   14
The Art of Not Having   16
States and Provinces   17
Waterfront Memoir   18
Another Dead-Wall Reverie   19
"A Calm Is No Joke"   20
Two Masters in a Museum   21
Naming the Dead   22
Death Penalty   24
For Martin Bergen   25
A Winter's Tale   26
The Guest in Room 217   27
The Women of Paradise Township   28
Author's Proofs   30

II. More than a metal

Cheerleaders Practicing in Eveleth, MN   33
On the Iron Range, Where I Tossed My First
  Book of Poems   34
Minnesota Shutdown   36
Afternoon Yard Sale on the Air   38
Miners   40
A Tale of Iron Range Luck   41
The Best Summer   43
Power Plant Dawn   45
The Solv-it-all Salesman at a Plant Safety Meeting   46
Five Magnesium Poems   47
Morning in Utah   53
Where Loneliness Broods   56

The Stillness of Certain Valleys   57
The Hot Times   58

III. Light after light

Light After Light   61
The Librarian of Everyday Life   63
American Idyll   64
One Night   65
The Unsuccess   66
What the River Said   67
In a Drug Store   68
Helping My Mother Move in   69
The Dogwoods   70
Good Shoes   71
Galileo's Daughter   72
Mothers' Day Meditation   73
Florsheims on All Saints Ave   74
New Year's Day, 2009   75
The Present   76
Two Women   78
Furnace Prophecy   79
Frank Little in the Big Sky State   80
Working Here   81

Acknowledgments   83

About the author   85

I. First check

David Salner

First Check

Fifteen years old. I'm staring at the check,
mesmerized by it, for it's more important
than my own hands, rubbed raw
from swinging a grass whip
through knee-high weeds all week.

I work with Sonny and Mac.
We're dripping with sweat by coffee break.
Sonny gives me the blow-by-blow
for every fight he's ever started.
Mac shows me a handshake with skin.

On Friday, in Baltimore, the eagle flies
through the chrome-colored skies
and the harbor air, freighted with cinnamon
from the grinding machines at McCormick Spice.
All summer long, the heat grinds on,

clouds turn amber from sulfur,
gray from the carbon at Sparrow's Point.
And the eagle flies at the Number Ten stops
and the pawn shops and package stores
full of laughing and crying men.

Laughing and crying, we work until three
and take the long walk back to the office,
timing our arrival for the precise moment
when Mr. Obitz, our pear-shaped boss,
has finished the weekly chewing out

and is handing out checks. I stare
at the name of the bank—*Fidelity Something*.
One man is dancing, one whispers sweet nothings
and kisses his check. Mac floats his in the air

and snags it with elegant nonchalance.

Sonny squirrels his away, fists up.
In my mind's eye, the three of us
are always receiving those checks —
through war, urban renewal and rebellion —
and in the whole city of Baltimore,

Fidelity Something no longer exists.

David Salner

Swimming the Severn

The river is half-salty, buoying him as he rolls
in its murkiness, snorts, and sneaks
a look at the dock he dove from, growing smaller
with each stroke. His sister is the little figure
with gold bangs, who clutches the hand
of their skinny father. The boy
should have told them before he dove in
that today he would swim the Severn. He pauses
midriver, hardly having to tread, keeping an eye
for motorboats, and seems to stand, cork-like,
half-way. He stares at the docks
jutting out from the green laurel brush
that stickers both banks. Equidistant,
he bobs in the light-brown mix, alert
to what people will say about him, this boy
who thinks he can swim like a man. Not a bad boy,
really, somewhere in between. Ahead,
the tan of the public beach. A big woman
in a black one-piece
gossips with a girl his age, who scowls
as he slips under the safety rope
and emerges among families he doesn't know.
Underfoot, sharp stones mixed with sand.
He walks from the water, between two boys
playing catch with a red and white ball,
who don't notice this stranger, this boy
who just swam the river and stands,
knee-deep, breathing heavily, now, licking
a trace of salt, diving back under the rope.

He's the boy who swam the river,
the one who worried his father
and little sister, those distant figures
waiting for him on the dock. No, he thinks,
I never meant to worry them, ever.

Working Here

As Far as He Dared

With each drawing he'd go
as far as he dared to the edge
before turning back. Once,
he ventured to the margin
of the world, as if he'd been
testing and found something
out there. It was weighty
and boundless, whatever it was,
scaring him into days of silence—
and then, his pen began sketching,
as far as he dared, again, drawing
plants and fingers with veins—
always a delicate line, connecting
the pained extremities. The lines
huddled together, faint creatures
at the edge of his thought. Each
waited for him, until one night
he never appeared to lead them back.

David Salner

The Welder on Midnight Shift

> *"That picture is the best attempt I have made to locate the center of interest by strong light."*
>
> – George Bellows on his painting, "The Excavation at Night"

It's only a pit, huge as the summer sky and deep,
where the new Penn Station is going up.

The beam of an arc light in the pit
finds tenement houses by mistake,

explores the facades, invades the windows,
and floods the rooms where people sleep.

They toss in the tide of light coming in
through windows open because of the heat,

while he burns holes on midnight shift,
feeding metal in with a little push

till it puddles up
in a dark corner of the pit. Our eyes

circle back to the work he does
in a halo of light his hands create.

Manhattan Seasons

summer
tomatoes
trucked in from Jersey
with a little dirt. Also,
romaine and dressing.
When I get back from Rockaway,
after I've gotten the sand out,
I'll wash them under cold water
and use a sharp knife.

fall
on my way home from work
I'll look for meat on sale
and something I can use
for a starch — coffee filters,
some brandy, and *The News*
so I can read about
a wide receiver's ACL.

winter
these old buildings
were built for Jewish immigrants.
Some facts are meat to chew on.
I'll slice the zuchini and onions
and then go out
for margarine,
a little hamburger,
and some aspirin.

spring
at the liquor store
that never opens its grating
I'll pick up something

David Salner

in a dry Chilean
then chick peas,
cucumbers, and peppers.
A clean breeze
flutters in the curtains.

The Art of Not Having

Improvising songs I thought you heard
when you rose like a diver in the air
and pressed your nose into a corner of the room.

So I remained, your straight-man in the dust,
to figure what I could of physics: Was it
intentional, and how should it be punished?

But your flesh shimmers like a language in the waves.
There are no waves.
I ask for no such dispensation.

David Salner

States and Provinces

In Arizona, we camped out
on a trail through the desert
beside the one and only tree.

In Utah, we went down
a northern slope in June
into an inch of snow.

In Idaho, by Hebgen Lake,
a man kept bringing us trout,
fillets the size of my feet.

In West Virginia, we trudged
through the wet shadows
of the mountain rhododendron.

We lay beside the Gulf
which was a *Curacao* blue
in the province of Quintana Roo.

Waterfront Memoir

From decktop, I see ships
nosing into piers — black flanks
high above the waterline. "Plenty of work
since Vietnam," an old guy says.

I scrape out ancient oil tankers,
breathe fumes all night until I'm dizzy.
I can barely climb the steel ladders
slick with condensate. The bay falls silent.

Pier 34 next morning. I walk the gangway
to another deck. I stand there
seven stories high, toss a smoke into the bay.
I show my orders to a red-faced man —

sharp beak, sarcastic scowl — and ask:
"Where's the Walking Boss of the Norway Gold?"
"Doesn't matter," comes the answer. "You'll work
unloading coffee in Number Two hold."

"Watch out for the winch operator,"
a voice crowds in. "He'll drop a load on you
and forget it by lunch."

A hundred-fifty pounds a bag.
Two men on a bag. Stab it with a baling hook.
Watch the green beans run.

They're calling numbers at the Scalers' Hall.
The a.m. board goes round and round.
There's work at every pier to Army Street,
where boxes big as tanks are sent
to Vietnam.
No blessing asked. None given.

David Salner

Melville: Another Dead-Wall Reverie

If I eat papaya and bittersweet chocolate
within an hour of bedtime, I'll dream
of sailing a catamaran beyond the reef
and into a sea too wide for my own good.
It's gentle, which can be deceiving.
A shot of gin and I'll dream of a pub
in London, circa 1835. Another shot
and I'll feel guilty, but—hell!
I'm a weaver in the mills, carrying the empire
all these years. I'll have another shot.
But when sheets of icy rain
fall on the city and the water courses, tea-brown,
down gutters and into sewers—
I realize that I'm susceptible
to a recurring dream in which a well-dressed chap
stares at me and pronounces the words,
"Ah, Bartleby! Ah, Humanity!"

"A Calm Is No Joke"

—Herman Melville, *Mardi*

A calm is a state of being
where being comes into doubt.
There was such a calm in my life, enforced
by lack of funds. I slept on a mattress
in a room the size of a closet. On the shelf—
a bag of rice, some pasta, five cans
of sauce, a gallon of cheap red wine.
I parceled it out one meal a day. Sometimes
I'd check if my buddy was tending bar—
a free drink here, a free drink there.

I laughed myself to sleep each night, musing that
according to string theory, a hamburger
was under my nose. I was flaky as rust,
going mad and loving it, just lying there,
Watching those cans of red sauce disappear.

When I got to the last one, I relaxed
and listened to the gray wings of a fly
inside my head. I knew it was a fly,
spiders are quiet as dust. *So what—*
I thought—even when the wine ran out.

One day, an envelope came in the mail—
manila, I had to sign for it—calling me
back to work, giving me just three days
to report. I shaved with a rusty blade,
begged a loan at the bar, ate a breakfast

of steak and eggs, and began to forget
my life without an edge, that blur, which
Melville called a calm. It had lasted a month.

David Salner

Two Masters in a Museum

> *"The depravity of the business classes of our country is not less than has been supposed but infinitely greater."*
> — Whitman

Two masters of industry, on parade
with their entourage, shoes squeaking hardly
at all, coughs muffled, with the decorum
we expect from the wealthy and well-bred--
until they come to the Flemish landscapes
by the master whose subject was always
punishment and damnation. See how the eyes
of the masters of industry twinkle
over the weird monsters and devices
designed to torture rebellious peasants.
Their eyes meet, like pickpockets in a crowd,
and they exchange a grin, without speaking,
but their inmost thoughts are amplified and heard.

Naming the Dead

> *— for the Forensic Team of Argentina, which has pursued its work throughout Latin America*

We descend on the scene with fine-haired brushes
and little pliers, cleaning and plucking like birds
over their young, collecting everything from teeth
in the dirt, to an old belt buckle
with the head of a horse, or a bald doll,
which is easier to identify than a little girl.

A coin glistens in the mud, balanced
on a femur. Cotton strands of a pocket
are dissolving around it, as if the power of X-ray vision
were sweeping across these muddy graves.

We have learned so far — from the location
of the hole in each skull — That these victims
were shot while being obedient children.
Now they can answer to given names.

Why do the next of kin
pursue the names of these little bones?
Why do they ask us to pull on our latex gloves
and sift the dirt from the sadness?

To identify this doll or this buckle?
To treasure this little plastic bag?

In the final interview, they thank us
with an almost stately composure
for we have been naming their dead
in fields, like this, beyond personal grief

David Salner

all over Latin America. Now, let us seek
the names of the murderers
and their advisors — distant, seemingly untouchable —
they, also, must be named.

Death Penalty

In a book of Mayan drawings
I saw the outline figure of a prisoner
who has been condemned to death.

He stands before the great ruler
and tears float like feathers
around his face. The two men

are identical
except for the tears.

David Salner

**For Martin Bergen, Hanged as a Molly Maguire,
January 16, 1879**

The rope takes hold, the body drops,
twists slowly, seems to pick up speed, to spin.
A Pottsville sheriff grabs the rope
to stop the spinning, saws him down.

"It happened last night," was all his son could think.
The boy went off to school that morning
too young to think of how the rope
had stretched an inch before it tightened.

Of all the things the father may have done
nothing compares in violence to this.
Twenty were hanged in Schuylkill County
before they got to him. He was the last one,

the one who had to wait.

A Winter's Tale

One night, when I lived in Cedar Rapids,
Big Al knocked at the door. The wind
came in from the river, which was frozen.
He asked me for twenty dollars—which was a lot
back then—because his wife needed medicine.

He promised to pay me back next Friday
at the bar, where he was a bouncer. I woke up
and went to the factory where I worked
and then to the bar, where Terry told me
Big Al hit him up for thirty. Then Snake,

the drummer, came in. He wouldn't say
how much he loaned Big Al. He crossed the dance floor
and tapped on his drums. Terry poured out two drinks
and said, "That's the last we'll see of Big Al."
We stared at our drinks. "Dave," Terry said,

"You shouldn't have fallen for that line
about Big Al's wife. He's not even married."
I didn't ask what line Big Al used on him.
"Hell, what's it matter," he said, as if he heard
what I thought, and we laughed. Then the door opened

and the wind came in from the frozen river.
It was Big Al. Tears streamed down his face.

David Salner

The Guest in Room 217

He was a famous investor, ruined by the market,
who came to the motel I worked at, Room 217.
When I found him, he was surrounded by pizza
and he had this look on his face
as if he was about to ask something like,

"Could you leave me an extra towel
and some shampoo?" The TV
was on the sports channel and the question
he never asked followed me as I went back
to the desk and called the police.

Perhaps he was going to ask me
something more important, but I hope not.

The Women of Paradise Township

As I grow older, they loom above me,
those women of Paradise Township — and now,
I live in their shadows — though they were
short women mostly. Like Mrs. Stambaugh,

Russell's mother, a woman bent
like a bucket handle, who outworked the sexton,
Russell's father, keeping the church so clean
that when the faithful died, they left the congregation

complaining of the housekeeping in heaven.
Or Mrs. Myers, Lonnie's mother, who showed me
the two huge hogs she was feeding and said:
"Smarter than any cow but heck to clean."

These women sliced hogs to cutlets, wrapped pork
in paper, then went out for sassafras, which grew wild
around their gardens, to make iced tea we drank all summer.
It had a yellow flower, faint and green,

and could be poisonous, but not in Mrs. Bentzel's hands.
She was Dean's mother. I still remember
how she sped into the field on a tractor,
holding her housedress above the axle, hollering,

"Your mom's up at the house — time to go home!"
Those women were married — all of them carried
their Mrs. like a sentence — except for a mother
and her daughter, at the elbow of a dirt and gravel lane

between the Staub farm and the church. They were
as nameless as the lane. My mother took pity on them,
tisking her lips that we, their closest neighbors, didn't
even know their names, couldn't put a face

David Salner

to their husbandless lives. Late that fall, we took off
for their cluster of shacks, which we could clearly see
now that the corn was down: barn, outhouse,
brick farm-house, with dry-rotting porch. I knocked,

holding a pie—the smell of cinnamon and apples
ascended in the huge November air. She answered
in a giant wrap with buttons, skin dry as chalk,
and a voice that struggled from a toothless mouth

that could have been a sink-hole in her face. "Wait there"—
she ordered—"I'll get my mother." And so I waited
for the mother of the oldest woman in the world.
All I can remember is that she'd aged

scarcely any better. Later, the neighbor-women told us
how they watched out for "those two girls."

**

Each fall, when the freeze begins to deepen,
I become a boy again, in a cornfield turned to stubble,
cloud-shadows flying, like the billowing house dresses
of the women of Paradise Township, passing over me—

Mrs. Stambaugh, Myers, Bentzel, and "those two girls"—
who traveled from kindness to kindness to a tough old age.

Author's Proofs

On p. 17, in the penultimate paragraph,
delete "hoped" and replace it with
my original sentence, "He lay on his cot,
not daring to hope"; replace the caption
on p. 21, "Dorothy Burnside, the heartthrob
of the Victorian era," with, "Admiral Herbert,
on his election to the House of Commons";
in the painting by Arnold, on p. 27, the green
in the grass is too robust, the wrong hue used
for the sunset; under the sketch on p. 81,
replace—"Antelope are often found
on the outskirts of this windblown town"—
with—"The oldest dinosaur
never saw a flower."

David Salner

II. More than a metal

Working Here

David Salner

Cheerleaders Practicing in Eveleth, MN

The sky is a stone-cold blue, a late-summer blue.

In the North Country, there are blues so perfect
you want to tear your heart out to be alive
and sober. And the cheerleaders of Eveleth High
are stamping their feet in the cinders, wearing
flip-flops, pumps, tennis shoes, sandals.

They maintain a businesslike, a gum-chewing calm
as they rehearse the difficult moves, like the toss,
which must be perfect, and the even more difficult catch—
with a strength not in their arms, which are slender, and not
in their conditioning, which is nonexistent. I don't

blame them. Last night was a good one to spend
on the lakes with their friends and a case of beer.
Those lakes, some glacial, some quarried out.
Those lakes in the North Country, that perfect sky—
it's enough to make you get sober or try

or cry. But when Shelly Jongewaard flies in the air,
she knows that whatever else in the rest of her life
could go wrong, and probably will, the arms
of those girls from Eveleth High will be there
beneath the stone-cold blue of the sky, the sober sky,

will always be there, locked in a basket to catch her.

On the Iron Range, Where I Tossed My First Book of Poems

I tossed my first book of poems into a trash can
outside a mine. It was a hot day — the book
stirred up yellow jackets feasting on soda cans.

So I hurried into the locker room, which we called
a "dry," because that's where our coveralls
hung from a chain in the ceiling, with the legs

outstretched like the skins of large animals —
still wet when we climbed back into them.
I worked in the mine, patrolling a rotary kiln,

the largest in the world, said the company.
All night it rolled like a great whale
in bearings the size of my house.

My partner told stories about the old days
when he drank at Tony's instead of going home
to sleep — and then passed out in the gray mud

under the filter floor. We laughed and talked
as the machines splattered mud all over us.
Later that winter — after the hunters

had divided the deer into neat packages
and the fishermen had begun putting wood stoves
into their ice-houses, and after the snowmobilers

had begun cruising under bridges
and into forbidden areas — I skied to the top
of an old tailings dump, where all I could see

David Salner

were Spruce and Tamarack rising from the stillness
of an ocean frozen under feet of snow
all the way to Lake Superior—a silent ocean

in which I could no longer hear the crushers
gyrating boulders of iron
at the edge of the sleepy town. Then Christmas:

U.S. Steel laid us off by the thousands,
and I left the Iron Range,
where I'd tossed my first book of poems.

Working Here

Minnesota Shutdown

I loafed that winter, burned the last of my wood,
skied over lakes, along endless power lines,
miles of desolation, towers of silence.

The great kilns cooled until spring, turned slowly
in a wildness of needles and vines.
The rock trucks, the forty-foot drills
were invisible, now. Aspen grew tall
along the chain fence surrounding the pit.
For the first time, the living-room sills
were clear of the grit from coolers and kilns.
Ivy scrawled over the benzene and tar.

I lived in a ruin overgrown, a paradise
of silent time. Where was the howl and screech
of a grate jammed with pellets on midnight shift?
The machines we tended, survived on, rebelled against,
rusted in weeds. Tough men and women began to leave.

That summer, I swam my heart out in the lake.
I fished for walleye, for fierce, oily pike.
At dusk, in the endless gray light,
mosquitoes feasted on ankles and hands,
on fat green veins. A giant in a gray business suit
banged his fist on my door. I snuck out
before he could serve the foreclosure notice.
I sold my canoe, stuffed my Plymouth Satellite
with everything else, headed down Route 35
to West Virginia, to a new power plant
where I swept fly-ash from concrete decks
around shiny, magnificent turbines. They spun so fast
a stillness overcame the motion.

David Salner

I checked call-backs for years.
I still heard the hiss of the load-out chutes,
saw the pellets of iron fill the rust-brown cars.

On those winter mornings, the pellets were hot
and steamed in the air. The sun was a marble of ice.
Mist trailed off the trains all the way to Duluth.

Afternoon Yard Sale on the Air

Even the desire for something old
gets old. I'm not in danger of buying
on my last day on the Iron Range, my truck radio
tuned to Afternoon Yard Sale. *One sofa, almost new,
never been sat on, $50, who wouldn't want
 to be the first?* I'm thinking of my first day
in the mines, as I drive past the lakes
full of walleye and northern pike. *Still available,
pocket knife, stainless steel with rosewood handle.*
I could spend more money on fishing rods
than I sold my good ones for. *Pressure washer,
fill dirt, plenty of fill. Steel lunch boxes —*
I remember them: deep-boxed, shiny,
held five, six sandwiches. We'd decorate them
with glossy labels from Lindy Gas, Auni Vulcanizing,
Clark Equip. We pasted Copenhagen ads on tool boxes.
One welder put up stickers for Ducks Unlimited and BASS
as if emblems of the outdoor life
could make the shift pass. It passed. Nothing new left
in Itasca or St. Louis counties. *Welders' beanies
with cheerful polka dots.* Can't pass them up, although
the last thing I need the day I leave
is polka dots. *Estate auction this Saturday,
complete untouched inventory from plumbing company
including back hoe, late model work van, and a warehouse
full of pipes and fittings. Contact B. Larew and Sons,
Auctioneers.* At one sale, I found fillet knives
up the wazoo. *Seventeen perfect games
have been pitched in the major leagues, and the people
at Eveleth Realty will pitch you a perfect deal,
so come on down to our office
beside the Foodland, and we'll help you connect
for all your mortgage needs, refinancing included.* Did good
selling my own stuff in a yard sale. *Ten white*

David Salner

nurses uniforms, extra large. Three months later,
bought back my outboard motor. *This Saturday,
another multifamily sale, 8 a.m. to 3 p.m.
in Aurora. The directions say drive into town
and look around. Lock tumblers, Timpken bearings,
and a watch, 17 jewels. Husqvarna chain saw. If it's
good enough for the trees in Sweden, should work here.*

The day before the shutdown, we threw a party,
and Halberg brought a gallon of Petri brandy.
Christ sake, Lampi said, you can't bring booze
on company property, want to get fired? We looked at him
and laughed and drank and put our safety locks
on everything. *Help wanted ads used to be next,
used to be, but today we'll sign off
with a message from Rev. Jasper Petterson
of Hibbing Lutheran. "I don't watch movies much,
but the Ten Commandments has to be the greatest.
I love how Charlton Heston waved his hand
above the Red Sea, and how the Hebrews
made a good escape, with Pharaoh breathing down their necks,
along a road of frozen waves
into a better day. . ."*

Working Here

Miners

Not proud or ashamed, just miners.
I changed out rollers, lying on my back
in frozen mud. I torched the rusted bolts
and watched a shower of sparks
sizzle on the ice.

During maintenance shutdowns, we put our safety locks
on everything that moved. Like ants,
we swarmed all over huge equipment. That's me,
on a mill the size of a bus, ten-pound hammer
clanging on a slug wrench.

When I said "miner,"
some people looked at me like I'd just said
"red ass of a baboon." They cut a wide swath, as if
the dirt under my nails might be contagious. Miners,
just miners. We were all laid off.

David Salner

A Tale of Iron Range Luck

Applying for work at U.S. Steel, a young man—Roger,
Arnold Maki's boy—passed a timber wolf beside the road
to Mt. Iron. A rare sight, even in the North Country,

and maybe a good omen, Roger thought. The wolf stared back,
as if wishing something other than good luck, and slipped
   away
into the spruce. Only the yellow eyes were left. Roger sped on,

safe in steel and glass, toward the stacks of the mining
   complex.
He got the job and celebrated his luck in the green and amber
   light
of Main Street and celebrated after each shift of numbing work

with the inner gladness of a good stiff drink. Christmas
   approached,
and an unfounded rumor niggled the labor gang, turned into
   news,
became an official letter that began, "Regretfully—"

Regretfully. After their unemployment had run out, the miners
still filled the bars but only in the daytime, began to piss away
the last of inner gladness. Domestic violence increased. On
   each stoop—

like lead, a block of government cheese was tossed. Rumors
   spread.
For example, Mrs. Engstrom heard it from a clerk who filed
   papers
in the inner sanctum that market conditions were about to
   change

Working Here

and everyone would get called back. No one believed it. First,
just a trickle, then a flood of miners left. An inner chill replaced
the gladness that a paycheck makes. That strip of ice and rock

was now devoid of youth. Well, almost. After all the others,
 Roger
decided to gun it out of town. That could be the end of story —
 but
does anyone who leaves such desolation not look back

without a sense that something could be out there, even worse?
Thick clouds, promising a winter storm, shrouded the moon
that night. Two yellow eyes were what he saw come after him.

David Salner

The Best Summer

He makes coffee and has the junkyard
all to himself. The sun dries out the steel hoods
as he stares at the tires sunk flat in the weeds
and stirs in sugar Business picks up around ten
as men come in with crescents of dirt
jammed under their nails, asking for a carburetor
from a late-eighties Dodge or a wiper motor
from a ten-year-old Ford. After work,
he picks up Alicia, and they go
to a flooded ore pit and swim to the center,
floating and racing, as the sun sets
behind the tall spruce. They tread water —
legs waving as though under glass —
and drift in circles around each other,
swimming back to the ledge,
pulling hand over helping hand — to emerge
and brush mosquitoes off each others' skin.
They put a towel on a shelf of stone
and make love, gulping air,
holding tight, falling back
while the sky darkens. They doze then sit up,
pull a six-pack of beer from the quarry
and whisper, till the night gets cold.

The following day, he dozes in the junkyard,
drinks coffee, reads the headlines about the new war,
and searches for a quarter panel from an old Monte Carlo.
On the way home, he stops at the army recruiter —
just to ask about the new war — and signs up. He doesn't
know why. "I just wanted to get it over,"
he says. "What over?" she cries. "Us? Our lives?"

Working Here

Next morning, he stares at the columns of cars
and imagines the drivers are here, each revving
their engines for someplace to go. After work,
he'll play basketball at the armory, then try
to make up. He'll tell her the rest of his dreams.
He spends the a.m. pulling an engine and picks up
the phone a couple of times. I must be crazy,
he thinks. This had been the best summer of my life

David Salner

Power Plant Dawn

I repaired equipment
large enough to sleep in,
honing plates of gray steel
in the chamber of a turbine
that supplied electric power
to eight states. Sometimes
I aligned a rubber belt
long as a river and wild.

At dawn, I took an elevator
to the top of a great stack
and stared from West Virginia
to Ohio, at another plant.
Its stack was a light tan stroke
painted on the morning sky
thirty miles away.

Fists around the railing,
I watched an opal mist
bury the trees and houses,
the large and tiny lives
being lived so far away.

Then I took the elevator
to the first floor and walked away
from the rumble of the pulverizers
and the chill of dew on steel
and drove down highway 64.

Working Here

The Solv-It-All Salesman at a Plant Safety Meeting

The doubts of these burly, irascible men —
that's what he wanted to put to rest.
So he held up a can of the solvent
he hoped to keep on selling in order to send
his daughters and son to various colleges.

"Safe enough to drink," he said of the stuff —
like that's all we needed to know —
and looked around the meeting, at little Arthur,
who weighed three-hundred pounds
and, for seven years, had washed his hands in it,

scrubbing the black and blue grease
from under his nails with an old toothbrush.
It left his skin pink and tingly. All of us
had been breathing it on the job for ages
and wanted to know about the skin rashes

we'd begun to develop — but the salesman
moved on to other topics, like industrial glues,
which he also sold. A pop-tab opened
and Manny offered a Pepsi — "on me!"
The salesman said "thanks!" took a swig,

and started to tell us of other safe products.
When Manny asked — "How's that soda?" —
the salesman grinned at first and then guessed
what was mixed in. Before our eyes, he changed
from a wise-cracking man. But I have to give credit

where it's due. He got a grip and finished his spiel
before hurrying off to the nearest men's room
in the foundry. We could hear him, above the squeal
of the cranes — in one of the stalls,
on the last day he sold Solv-It-All.

David Salner

Five Magnesium Poems

1. Sketch of a bus ride to graveyard shift

The diesel motors on US Route 80
sound almost human as they whisper, laugh,
grow angry and pass in a scream of lights
as we sway on the shocks of an old school bus.

The tracks of the Union Pacific railroad speed by
and the Salt Lake glows in a silver light
as the night breeze brushes the dead sea water
into waves that lap at the ballast and ties.

My headphones carry bluegrass —
an old man with emphysema, singing
into the everlasting night. He's answered
by my face in the window. I stare through myself

into the darkness of a salt marsh, with weeds
sharp enough to draw blood and biting flies.
The wreck of the Morton Salt Building floats by,
then a sign that reads: When it rains it pours.

Then rain,
drenching and peaceful, nothing but rain.

Working Here

2. Sketch of the passengers

> "Deep in their hearts they remember hell."
> — Beowulf

I sleep for a while and then wake up
on a bus ride, with twenty-eight men
all wishing they had a seat to themselves —
except for two brothers, the Shingeldeckers.
Their shoulders bump like waves in the ocean.

There's Staz, who organized miners
in the copper district of Poland: "I knew Lech
before he sold out." No surprise. No disappointment.
And now — with his lungs full of chlorine gas
from this plant in Utah — no hope.

Adams — an electrician —
came to work on the Great Salt Flats
after his brother and twenty-six others
burned to death in the Wilberg mine.
The name of his hometown is Helper, Utah.

—And the prisoners we pick up in Tooele.
They hate the work, but it gets them key privileges.
Some go drinking, instead, and wake up
on the floor of the county jail, still drunk
but happy to miss a shift in the foundry.

Richard, a Goshute Indian,
has a rightful claim to this land.
As a boy, he played in Skull Valley,
on these salt flats, surrounded
by orange cliffs. His family

48

David Salner

went to court to save their land
but lacked proof of title. After all,
who could a Goshute family
say they bought this land from —
the night sky? the stars?

Working Here

3. Magnesium furnaces

— for Willie and others

From the Great Salt Lake, a reckoning
of ancient salts, whose sea is now.

Each furnace gleams at 1300 f, a blood-red pool,
but when the temp goes up just ten degrees,
the red salt burns, scabs over like a child's skin.

Change out a pump, the mag ignites
into a star-size sparkler
for one heart-stopping, incandescent moment
in the barn-dark night.

Gag on the beautiful fumes
of sulfur and chlorine, drown in gems
of precious sweat, as you stack ingots, 30-lbs each,
for a 12-hour shift.

A casting machine shrieks and you shriek back —
flexeril, skellaxen, bachoffen,
naproxen, neuroten, oxychontyl.

David Salner

4. Rage

– for John Langford

More than a metal,
mag comes from ponds near the Great Salt Lake
and brews in a ramshackle factory
prickling with magnetism and brown with rust.

We cast mag into ingots slippery as brine
and grab them with steel handles.
We stack ingots until our coveralls
are caked with salt—so we can make

mag cheap enough for pop tabs
and racing wheels. Shift after shift
Mag sucks its value from us,
but we are the ones transformed.

More than a metal, we cast these ingots
from a rage of lightning.

Working Here

5. The lights from the bars in Magna, Utah

> *— for Dave Harding*

Just south of Route 80
the lights from the bars of Magna, Utah,
light up the desert night with amber.

After my midnight shift,
I stop at Dave Harding's bar.
Dave worked at the plant — until he got sick.
Now, he serves eggs and ham steaks
as thick as my thumb, with a set-up.
I bring the gin in a brown paper bag.

Dave's face, always flushed,
shines from behind the bar, like the bottles
nobody orders — Chivas, Grand Marnier, and Tanqueray.

I have a few drinks, tell him about work.
His face lights up as he tells me the news —
his doctor has filed court papers.
The fluid in his lungs and his swollen heart
come from breathing the gas at work.
"Good news," Dave says.
"Now we can get those company bastards."

Dave goes off to pour beer,
and I wait while the rest of the crew shoots pool
for him to come back. It's a shift work crowd.
Who cares what the sun is doing outside.

That was late fall. The following year
Dave died of pneumonia at age 35.

Morning in Utah

> — *for Carl Burnett*

1. A Tale

Carl has a purpose in life
as worthy as yours or mine.

He tells the foundry new-hires
a tale, how a furnace blew up
burning everything on the fork truck—
hydraulic lines, dash, even the seat
the operator sat on—
to a crisp.

It's a cautionary tale
to instill safety consciousness.

Carl tells us the final part, too—
how the operator
never lost consciousness
and spoke to his brother
from a bed in University Hospital
for hours.

Carl can't tell us
what the two brothers talked about
in the room where their voices
spilled over each other
like rough-housing boys.

Working Here

2. Punching in

A tendril of orange gas
seeps from a corrugated roof.

I grab my safety equipment
and head for the building I work in —
a respirator hanging from my index finger
like a dead reptile.

When I press it to my face,
it gives me the sour kiss
of rubber put away wet.

I can work when the gas is saffron
but when it turns neon
I'll puke my guts out.

The pay isn't great
but here I find
a whiff of eternity
or at least the stink of hell.

David Salner

3. Punching out

Driving home from the magnesium plant,
I can see a pale light behind the mountain
where Big Bill Haywood mined silver
a century ago — and they mine it there still
whenever the price goes high enough.

I stay on Route 80, pass the copper smelter,
circle the open-pit mine, and enter
a valley of landfill and loam. To the south,
Geneva Steel — a city unto itself
of roofs and fires —
blackens the horizon.
In Emery County, to the Southeast,
coal belts clatter nonstop.

On the north side of town,
by the vessels and stacks at Chevron,
a cracker shoots flames in the air.

At Flying J,
a contractor explodes while welding pipe.

It's morning in Utah —
the end of another midnight shift.

Where Loneliness Broods

At the West Valley flea market
loneliness broods in the collectibles.

Under the arch of an abandoned drive-in.
a man collects dollars and hands out tickets
for flea market parking and a lucky drawing.
But even the tools go begging: An almost new set—
one-inch drive ratchet and sockets—
the Sears catalog lists it for ninety
but I'll let it go for. . .

They came to West Valley from coal camps
in Price and Rock Springs, bringing their stories.
That woman selling quilts could tell you
how she cooked beans to feed three families
for a whole winter; the man passing out handbills
for a massage and tanning studio
pulled his friend from a burning mine.

A man selling belt-buckles
croons a line from Waylon Jennings
in a teardrop tenor—I've always been crazy.
The notes rustle deep in his lungs.

He scrapes a match on his fingernail
as the sun sets behind the Oquirh mountains,
and a shadow sweeps over the West Valley flea market
like the wave of a long-forgotten sea.

David Salner

The Stillness of Certain Valleys

The miners who worked here
lived in a town of clapboard and tar.
They ran coal into cars of dark iron
stretching for miles along the river.
Day and night the coal clattered down.
Black clouds rose the length of the valley.

Now, water drips from a tipple
to wild strawberries in the rail-bed below.
Someone has stacked the ties by the roadside.
Here and there, scavengers have been at it,
salvaging copper from cables, gathering
sections of belt, finding more trouble

than they can haul off. A jungle of ferns
smothers the old blockhouse of the fan.
Once it drew air, so the valley could live—
huge drafts of coal dust, methane, and rage.
The metal lungs never stopped breathing,
until this stillness entered the valley,

of weeds and rust. You can always hear
the underground voices, doggedly calling.

The Hot Times

The first time I saw molten steel
it looked like a yellow lake.

We were specters, haunting the steel,
dissolving in its light
then pouring out. Carbon specks,
discernible in heat after heat.

On a long weekend in December,
we went shopping downtown
and the streets were full of lights —
some red, some green, some white
as the steel I cast. When I went back
to the hot end, I got the news
the foundry was laying us off.

They put four-by-eight sheets
over shop windows.
Spring arrived like a trailer of scrap.

The hot times were over.

III. Light after light

Working Here

David Salner

Light After Light

— for Barbara, Brunswick, MD.

At four a.m. the first train rattles
the glazed windows in our apartment
by the tracks. I pack my lunch
and scrape the frost off my windshield
under the street lamps of this railroad town.

Someone is singing Nine-Pound Hammer
on the radio. I cross more tracks
and climb a ridge of South Mountain
where blue and gray-clad bodies
still huddle around trees and large stones.

I see the first light behind a woods
on a hillside in Pennsylvania and slow
for a speed trap as I enter town.
I drop two quarters for *The Herald*,
which has a headline on the price of milk,

and nod at the guard before entering
the lighted space in an old factory
large as a prison. Two mill-operators
are drinking coffee, and one of them
says what she knows about layoffs

in a voice that runs on rapidly
and then searches for the right words.
After my shift I roll down the windows
and cross back into Maryland, studying
the mixture of neat and shabby farms.

A Mennonite woman is riding a tractor
turning the gray field into dark rows

she will plant next spring.
In town, I stop at the liquor store
so we can sit outside and drink wine

as the trainmen switch cars
in the darkness. We talk for hours
as their clipped voices
say just what they have to
over the static of the radio.

David Salner

The Librarian of Everyday Life

To hell with the Dewey Decimal System
and those faint numbers on spine after spine!
Let's read the people, instead — like the old man
who is lifting to the check-out counter, with all his strength,
a volume called *Stay Young, Lift Weights*. The next patron
returns a book called *The Face of God* and the latest issue
of *Runners World*. As closing approaches,
the lights flicker in warning, and the librarian
knows who will emerge from the shadows
of fiction, from between shelves laden with
mystery and romance, the two basic genres
of everyday life. Now comes the jewel — the secret life
of this man. His co-workers on night-shift
consider him stuffy and boring — but the librarian
gets to place a card in his book and steal a glimpse
at the title: *Liberating Your Inner Comedian*.

American Idyll

We knew it was his job to be
mean, but did he have to be
that mean? The Judge had
led her on, saying: "The thing
about a voice like yours is that
no matter what you sing" —
and pausing just long enough
for her to hope — "It sounds
like crap." Her guitar sagged
from her arm, and we knew
even a Judge has no right
to be that mean. We started to boo —
we booed the Judges, the network,
and the ads. We booed until
her shoulders straightened
and her hand slid down
the throat of her guitar, and
she opened with the chords
of the only song we had to hear,
and then she sang into the very
darkness of our lives, Love Me
Tender — and tender was more
than a word, it was a way
things ought to be .... The last
note died away, she bowed
toward us, leveled her gaze
at the Judge, whose eyes tried
to say I'm sorry. She looked at him
and grinned, she just grinned.

David Salner

One Night

> *"If you love without evoking love in return...*
> *your love is . . . a misfortune."*
> — Karl Marx

Jason wore pearl-white chinos, and Shannon
was in brand new jeans, just tight enough
to show off her figure. They met at the party
of a mutual friend, in South East DC, laughed
at each other's jokes, and then slipped off
to his place for nightcaps. He woke up in bed
with her, half dreaming, convinced he'd gone
to heaven that night. The alarm went off
at 6:00 a.m., but she was already sitting up,
back to him, trapezoids flexing and knotting,
as she fastened her bra in front, then slid it
around and poked her arms through the straps.
She moved with a restlessness — a rippling
palisade of ribs beneath skin. Against this,
he murmured vague words that included —
"last night . . . really great" — while she put on
her shoes and stood up. "I want to see you
again," he blurted out. Not turning around,
she shot back, "I might call you —" although
she didn't even have his number. And so
this woman, who was prepared by everything
in her life to fall for this man, could not.
And this man, for whom falling in love
wasn't an option, found he was trapped. Why
does it work that way — as if feelings were
numbers on a wheel — the wrong one comes up?
Without a goodbye, without turning around,
she escaped his apartment, hardly leaving
a trace — but leaving this shaken man, naked,
still catching his breath in bed but needing
to hurry up, now, or be late for work.

The Unsuccess

A mirror hangs over the bar, showing me
a big man on a stool, seating himself
with some difficulty. Now we're shoulder to shoulder,
two beefy men. He's probably a salesman, after a day
of nibbles and no bites; I'm a steelworker, tired out
and ready to drink. He's the well-dressed one.

He grins nervously and seems to be in need
of saying something deeper than I want to hear.
"I've had a lot of unsuccess," he says.
Why not just say *failure?* I ask myself.
He orders a round for both of us. "Thanks," I grunt,
not exactly pleased to be sharing a drink
with a man whose unsuccess is so apparent.
I catch another glimpse of the two men in the mirror,
shoulder to shoulder. "No failures, *per se*,"
he says, a little loud above the music, "but a lot
of unsuccess. It's like when you play basketball as a kid —
you're never going to become Allen Iverson, ever,
so you could hardly be classed a failure when you don't,
despite the years of practicing fakes and no-looks.
The way things worked out —" and here he pauses
for his voice to tighten like a wrench
over the syllables — "I was a major unsuccess."
His fingers drum the bar beside his drink.
"My wife is cooking dinner," I tell him,
my shoulders conveying the apology. "Thanks for the drink."
The barstool squeaks, as I stand up,
hold the last of my watery drink before my eyes,
in a gesture more heartfelt, toss it down.
"I've had my share of unsuccess," I nod at him
and leave. "I could write a book about it."

David Salner

What the River Said

You can't step into the same
river twice—the philosopher said—
but did you ever wonder what
the river thought? Am I not
the same river today as I was
yesterday? Philosophers,
on the other hand, change
one moment to the next.
A river can never flow past
the same one twice. Take
Heraclitus. He had affairs.
Sometimes he was gay,
sometimes straight. Sometimes
he was with the people,
sometimes with the merchant class.

I can remember the day he told
his friend, bet you can't step into
that one twice, pointing at me,
toward a muddy bank, toward
turtles staring from the mud
and weeds with their hooded,
bewitching eyes. Twice? If he'd
have stepped into a river even
once, he'd have been a better man
for it. Invariably, I stretch out
between the banks of my friend,
whom you know as The Earth.
All night long, she tells me jokes.
All summer, all summer night long,
you should hear this river laugh.

Working Here

In a Drug Store

"Really, we can never relinquish anything."
— Freud

I wait for my prescription, ambling
around the vitamins and dental floss
until I get to the rack with the canes.
I turn to see if anyone is watching
before I pick one up and examine
the adjustable shaft and the holes
with the retractable peg. I feel
the coolness of the metal and lean
on it a little, surprised. By this time
I no longer care who's watching,
for I'm walking past the foot powder
and those pads you put in your shoes,
to the photo counter, at the far end
of the store. I pause and my face
relaxes, for I have the hang of it,
yes. I turn and start walking back
past the candy and greeting cards
to the rack with the other canes.
I feel the grip, again, and peer
at the price tag. Then the pharmacist
calls my name and holds out a bag
with the Rx. Not giving up anything,
really, I put the cane back.

David Salner

Helping My Mother Move in

It's Wednesday, and I've taken the day off work
to help my mother move in
to her new place, where people have forgotten

the "I" in I live here. I bring in a straw basket
and lift out the figurine of an ivory man.
and place him on a shelf between two plates.

The dull and lovely pewter of the plates —
they form a bas-relief with the ebony cranes
that stretch their necks into long shrieks.

I put the artificial flowers beside the bed,
and a woman enters in a faded house dress
asking if I've seen two Jewish children.

"I did not abandon them," she swears.
The spring wind
whips sheets of light through the nets of the mind.

It's Wednesday, and I've taken the day off work.
I did not abandon them.
I, of all people …

The Dogwoods

I loosen the fan motor on a wrecked Ford,
among acres of junk cars, in a landscape
of dead earth--and then I look up, there,
at the insouciance of the white flowers,
a dogwood in the spring breeze. And,
there, as those boys practice dribbling--
cross-overs, through-the-legs, no-looks--
another breaks out in provocative blossoms
and brushes the tarpaper roof of a shed,

for the dogwoods are flowering
this quick spring.

Good Shoes

Good shoes, all of us need good shoes,
for they support us — ankles, shanks,
even our elbows when we dance,

and the voice at the very top,
the words, the don'ts and dos,
all of it rests on good shoes.

Working Here

Galileo's Daughter

After her labors, she sits in the garden,
eating preserves made from the oranges
her father gave her, wondering
if everything she has thought and loved
dissolves into a history
that is dissolving. Beyond this dark
there is the sun her father proved,
the avoidless sun. But in this garden,
it is the taste of orange preserves
around which everything turns.

72

David Salner

Mothers' Day Meditation

Every time she lifts Lenaya from the crib,
she loses her place

in the book she's reading, on slavery,
on the lives of those women who were kidnapped

into—"Wait!"
—she yells out—because the big one, Little Keeshawn,

has toppled the trash-can on the floor—
egg shells, bread crumbs, and some red jello

she forgot she made. As she gets up to clean,
she puts Lenaya down, still lifting

the weight she gained to have her, imagining
she's balancing on the planks of that ship

surrounded by sharks
who curse her from the blood-red surf

for not jumping in like the rest.

Just for Lenaya and Little Keeshawn,
she clings to that oak and pine deck, taking

full face the spit of the waves, thinking,
"We make it to land—then what?"

Florsheims on All Saints Ave.

What made him surrender these shoes
and this jacket, which can still be purchased
from the flea market on All-Saints Ave? Why
were the blue serge pants removed, one leg
at a time, from this Florsheim man, this blue serge man?

Perhaps, as these discarded dress clothes suggest,
he walked the streets addressing those he met
as sir or ma'am, craving mutual respect, like some men
crave wine, women, or weed. Of these four things,
we should add, most men are in some kind of need.

The heels are worn on the outside but still good,
an inch thick, and the soles — God bless them —
are thick as well. The leather is shiny where the toes
ought to be, puffed out and stretched like the cheeks
of a boy, holding his breath against great odds.

What child, what man will never
kick up his heels in them?

David Salner

New Year's Day, 2009

Each New Year's Day,
I wake up a little earlier,
a little less hung over,
until today, no headache
at all. I make coffee,
turn on the news to see
the walls of a hospital
in Gaza exploding. I guess
one nation, at least,
decided against that
resolution: peace on earth.

Working Here

The Present

You always write about the past — why don't you write about the present sometime?

Is such a thing even possible?
The present? When I try to find it, I find
something else, like an old man looking for his keys
and finding a photograph of his daughter
when she was a child. I guess she was the Pumpkin Princess
that Halloween. Now I have forgotten
what I was looking for — Oh, yes! —
The keys! We all know what Heraclitus said
about the water of the present,
how you cannot submerge yourself in it
for it flows past, scatters and gathers, approaches
and departs. And St. Augustine argued that the present
must be durationless,
since an interval of any duration
can always be divided
into future and past. Sandwiched between them
lies the domain of the present, like the space between
two slices of bread
before the loaf is cut. But when you sit in the kitchen,
and I lean down and brush my lips
along your neck for a discreet moment
I'm definitely aware of and slide my hands
down your back and under your arms,
until I'm holding your breasts —
the present seems to spread out
willing and persuasive,
spilling like the oil of time, anointing
the space between past and future

David Salner

with an instant that grows into
this burst of endlessness
this moment
now

The present = eternity where there is no passage of time, or at least no experience of the passage of time, as in good love-making,

Two Women

After a winter storm,
after the wind dies down
and the air fills with a fine
white ash from people beginning
to shovel out because, after three
cups of coffee, they want to be
moving somewhere—a cry
breaks the spell, an old woman
breaks into the powder of the day.
Barbara, my wife, runs to her
and takes her hand, although
she doesn't know her at all,
and together they enter
the living room, where a man
lies on a cot, in nice pajamas,
buttoned to the throat, like the star
of a '40s movie, almost elegant
in his stillness. He stares
through the door and beyond,
at the dust-sized snow.
His last image—if he'd
have lived five minutes longer—
would have been these two women,
his wife and a total stranger
who just came in on a winter day
to remove his glasses
and brush down the lids of his eyes.

David Salner

Furnace Prophecy

I used to look through an open door
at a circle of white-hot steel, surrounded
by the empty foundry on night-shift, echoes
in rafters, pigeons in flue dust, a darkness
of unspeakable magnitude, and a furnace,
growing on a yard full of scrap, growling
with each oxygen blast, devouring
what we throw of chromium and mag, until
we tap it, and this scintillating disc
overdazzles the midnight expanse
of graveyard shift. The sun leaps
and flashes in the darkness
of my green visor. Of life and death,
of the great battle not yet begun,
I have at least this prophecy
to dazzle me — a midnight sun.

Working Here

Frank Little in the Big Sky State

They beat him, because it was clear
as moonlight to them that their fists
had the right to break a man's jaw
and muddy his flesh and blood
with their blows; then they tied him
to the bumper and dragged him
out of town, because it was a right
the darkness bestowed, and also
it was a nice touch, it was, to erase
a man's knees; and then they flung
a rope over an iron trestle and pulled,
all six of them, because at night,
they had the right to lift a man,
hand over hand, out of his life
on earth and into the big sky —
but before doing that, they had
the foresight to pin to his shorts
a sign warning us they knew who
we were and we could be next —
as the hills and buttes were their
witness, they had the right.

The next morning, we found him
cinched to the sky and cut him down
and claimed him
because it was our right
and buried him beneath red roses
and threw away the sign.

David Salner

Working Here

People who don't work here
would never dream
what it takes to make iron.
That's what we said at Eveleth Mines.

We walked a mile of coal-belts
to the tipping point, stared seven-stories down
into a shaft of air suffused with coal,
into the softness of slaked air.

On kiln patrol, marbles of iron
tumbled in a yellow ooze. The heat of hell
turned inches from our heads.
Then we paced a grate the size of a football field

to check each Atlas bearing
with something like a stethoscope
and listen for a telltale scratch
in the forever rolling of the world.

Or, we watched magnetic separators,
the red cones churning through a river
of gray ore. In the West Pit,
the bucket of a loader

brushed boulders of ore, a finger-flick.
But something about the crusher bothered us.
All over Northern Minnesota, it kept the earth awake,
shift after shift—until they shut it down,

and the whole expanse of grinding and breaking
ground to a halt. Then, everything was quiet
as an April snow. In all the bars,
a distant chatter, a sort of silence.

Working Here

Rumors they'd be calling back
to Eveleth Mines. Rumors, then more silence.
I think back to the noisy world I kept alive
when I did things you'd never dream.

That's what it took to make iron.

David Salner

Acknowledgments—

Appalachian Journal	"The Solv-it-all Salesman at a Plant Safety Meeting," "For Martin Bergen," and "Power Power Plant Down."
Atlanta Review	"Furnace Prophecy"
Bap Quarterly	"The Librarian of Everyday Life"
Beltway Poetry Quarterly	"Manhattan Seasons"
Borderlands	"The Stillness of Certain Valleys"
Boxcar Poetry Review	"Frank Little in the Big Sky State"
Clackamas Literary Review	"A Winter's Tale"
Common Ground Review	"Florsheims on All Saints Ave"
Confrontation	"First Check"
Cutthroat	"Magnesium Furnaces"
Delaware Poetry Review	"The Present"
Elixir	"A Dead-Wall Reverie"
Ekphrasis	"The Welder on Midnight Shift"
Evansville Review	"The Women of Paradise Township"
5 am	"The Dogwoods"
Free Lunch	"Naming the Dead" and "The Hot Times"
Goodfoot	"In a Drugstore"
Hubbub	"A Tale of Iron Range Luck"
The Iowa Review	"American Idyll" and "States and Provinces"

Isotope	"Waterfront Memoir"
King Log	"Where Loneliness Broods"
Leviathan: A Journal Of Melville Studies	"Another Dead-Wall Reverie" and "A Calm Is No Joke"
Minnesota Review	"The Best Summer"
North American Review	"The Art of Not Having"
Poet Lore	"One Night" and "Working Here"
Poetry Northwest	"Minnesota Shutdown"
Potomac Review	"Mothers' Day Meditation"
Southern Humanities Review	"Cheerleaders Practicing in Eveleth, MN"
Spillway	"Rage"
13 Miles from Cleveland	"Miners"
Threepenny Review	"As Far As He Dared"
Upstreet	"Author's Proofs"
WordTech	"A Dead-Wall Reverie" and "Rage"

Poems in this collection also appeared previously in chapbooks published by March Street Press and Pudding House. The author would like to thank the Maryland State Arts Council and the Puffin Foundation, Ltd., for grants that helped keep body and soul together while some of these poems were being written.

David Salner

About the Author—

David Salner completed an MFA degree at the University of Iowa Writers' Workshop and then worked for twenty-five years as an iron ore miner, furnace tender, and laborer. The people he knew during these years had a deep influence on his writing. He believes that "poetry, first and foremost among art forms, derives its creative impulse from the lives of ordinary working people. It should be a lively art form, based on the good nature and genius of humanity."

He is the author of three chapbooks and one previous book, *John Henry's Partner Speaks.* His work has appeared in many journals, including *North American Review, Threepenny Review, The Iowa Review, Poetry Daily, Prairie Schooner, Witness,* and *The Georgia Review.* He has been awarded grants from the Puffin Foundation and The Maryland State Arts Council, received two Pushcart Prize nominations, and the 2010 Oboh Award for poetry.

Now semi-retired, Salner divides his time between writing and volunteer editorial work in support of working-class causes. He lives in Frederick Md. with his wife, Barbara Greenway, a high school English teacher. They go fishing, spend more money than they make, and look forward to visits with their daughter, Lily.

Made in the USA
Middletown, DE
13 July 2015